Start to Learn
Animals

Green Android

Created and produced by:
Green Android Ltd
49 Beaumont Court
Upper Clapton Road
London E5 8BG
United Kingdom
www.greenandroid.co.uk

ISBN 978-1-909244-17-7

Copyright © Green Android Ltd 2013

Acknowledgements

Images © dreamstime.com: bengal tiger © Beetle2k42; falcon © Jordache; komodo dragon © Rokro; lion © Starletdarlene; piranha © Moori; polar bear © F2.

Images © flpa.co.uk: blue whale © Richard Herrmann/Minden Pictures/FLPA; leopard corydoras © Gerard Lacz/FLPA; octopus © Brandon Cole/Biosphoto/FLPA; sailfish © Reinhard Dirscherl/FLPA.

Images © fotolia.com: atlas moth © ksena32; brown bear © byrdyak; budgerigars © jagodka; butterflies © cynoclub; butterflyfish © bluehand; centipede, emu, poison dart frog © Eric Isselee; chihuahua © zothen; colorado beetle © Marianne Mayer; cuttlefish © Mexrix; dragonfly © M.R. Swadzba; ducks © fotomaster; earthworm © Spencer Berger; emperor moth © JPS; fish © Richard Carey; frog © Sascha Burkard; goldfish © Irochka; goose © DenisNata; goose © yevgeniy11; hens © sval7; labradoodle © biglama; leopard gecko © Thomas Beitz; llama © Vladimir Melnik; millipedes © James Steidl; moreidol © Ian Scott; mosquito © Henrik Larsson; ostrich © sirylok; pangolin © petert2; pig © spinetta; rabbit in a burrow © stanley45; rooster © Anatolii; salamander © Ionescu Bogdan; scorpion © asbtkb; sea slug © Neil Atterbury; seahorse © Onkelchen; seahorse © RbbrDckyBK; stag-beetle © fpainter7; stingray © crisod; tang © aquapix; turkey © Noo; walrus © MAK.

Images © shutterstock.com: alligator © Raffaella Calzoni; amazon milk frog, anteater, bearded dragon, chimpanzee, frill-necked lizard, hedgehog with baby, helmeted guinea fowl, hen, king cobra, kookaburra, milk snake, otter, porcupine, rabbit, rabbit and kit, raccoon, red palm weevil, scarlet Ibis, shetland pony, skunk, tomato frog, violet-backed Starling, zebra finch © Eric Isselee; angelfish © Johannes Kornelius; ant © Andrey Pavlov; anteater © Christian Musat; appaloosa horse © Makarova Viktoria; arctic fox © outdoorsman; armadillo © Steve Bower; axolotl, cockatoo © Andrew Burgess; baby Tawny owl © Florian Andronache; bald eagle © Richard Lowthian; bat © Sementer; bee © MPanchenko; bernese mountain dog puppies © steamroller_blues; bernese mountain dog, border collie © Erik Lam; bison © Zack Frank; black rhino © john michael evan potter; blue mountain butterfly © chungking; blue starfish © paul cowell; blue tit © Alexander Erdbeer; blue-tongued skink, jackson's chameleon, tigerfish, veiled chameleon, wood turtle, yellow tang © fivespots; bluejay © Mike Truchon; bongo © Andreas Gradin; brown bear © Jamen Percy; brown snake © Stephen B. Goodwin; buffalo © trevor kittelty; bull © Niar; butterfly © Perig; butterfly on the bark © Wilm Ihlenfeld; buzzard © BogdanBoev; caiman © sohadiszno; camel © alersandr hunta; canaries © ene; cane toad © Chris Ison; cat and kitten © Liliya Kulianionak; caterpillars © Ivanova Natalia, Ziga Camernik; cheetahs © Erwin Niemand, Mark Beckwith; chicks, wood mouse, pig © Tsekhmister; chinchilla © Steshkin Yevgeniy; chipmunk © Tom Reichner; clouded yellow butterfly © jesper skov; clown fish © Sergey Novikov; clown fish, jellyfish © Kletr; cockatiel © Marina Jay; cockroach © seeyou; common toad © Vishnevskiy Vasily; copperhead snake © Rusty Dodson; corn snake © Kruglov_Orda; cows © tarczas; coyote © Birdiegal; crabs © Eugene Sergeev, haveseen; crocodiles © froe_mic, nattanan726; dalmation © Susan Schmitz; deer © Ekaterina V. Borisova; devil scorpionfish © Kristina Vackova; discus © Andrey Armyagov; dolphins © aldorado, Tory Kallman, Paul Vinten; donkey © PD Loyd; duck and ducklings © Ewa Studio; dung beetle © r.classen; eagle-owl © Medvedev Vladimir; eastern collared lizard © Matt Jeppson; echidna © clearviewstock; eel © Pavel Vakhrushev; elephants © Dmussman, Patryk Kosmider; elephant and calf © Four Oaks; emerald tree boa, gecko © ChameleonsEye; emu © S.Cooper Digital; eyelash pit viper © worldswildlifewonders; fairy basslet © Stubblefield Photography; fawn © WilleeCole; fennec fox © Cat Downie; ferret © sbko; fire bellied toad © Michelle D. Milliman; fish © mexrix; flamingo © Atthapol Saita; frog swimming © gradi1975; gaur, hippopotamus, meerkats © tratong; gerbil © Anna Kucherova; gibbon © rujithai; giraffes © Joel Shawn, nelik; golden dart frog © reptiles4all; goldfish © Sergii Figurnyi; gorilla © Rudy Umans; goslings, ginger cat © oksana2010; grasshopper © cristi180884; gray african parrot © Richard Susanto; gray squirrel © Tony Campbell; great crested newt © JGade; great horned owl © csterken; great white shark, elephant and calf © Mogens Trolle; green anole lizard © Leigh Prather; green chameleon © Fedor Selivanov; green fly, wasp © irin-k; green ghromis, cardinal fish © Johannes Kornelius; green iguana © Nneirda; green tree python, victoria crowned pigeon © apiguide; guinea pigs © xstockerx, Vasily Kovalev; hammerhead shark © frantisekhojdysz; hamster © Subbotina Anna; harlequin poison frog, leaf mimic katydid © Dr. Morley Read; hedgehog © Zayats Svetlana; hens © Valentina_S; heron © AngelaLouwe; horse galloping © Olga_i; house spider © Sean Gladwell; hummingbird © kojihirano; humpback whale © David Ashley; ibex, water skater © Vadim Petrakov; iguana © granat; impala © Stacey Ann Alberts; jaguar © stephen; kangaroo © Kristina Postnikova; kangaroo with baby © idiz; kingfisher © assoonas; koala © worldswildlifewonders; korhaan © Daleen Loest; ladybird © Palto; ladybug © Yellowj; lantern fly © takepicsforfun; leaf cutter ant © Micha Klootwijk; leaf insect © kamnuan; leafy seadragon © Joy Brown; leopard frog © Gerald A. DeBoer; leopard shark © AdStock RF; leopard tortoise © Praisaeng; lion © Maggy Meyer; lions fighting © Tobie Oosthuizen; marbled newt © raulbaenacasado; moose, brown bear, storks, leopard, badger © Eduard Kyslynskyy; mossy frog, wood borer beetle © alslutsky; mountain hare © Peter Wey; mouse © Kuttelvaserova Stuchelova; muskox © Cornflower; northern cardinal © Jeffry Weymier; orangutan © Matej Hudovernik; orangutan and baby © Gabriela Insuratelu; orca © Christopher Meder; ornate horned frog, red poison strawberry frog © Dirk Ercken; oryx © Johan Swanepoel; ostrich © Sam DCruz; panda © Hung Chung Chih; parrot © elnavegante; partridges © Mircea BEZERGHEANU; pelican © iliuta goean; penguins © Neale Cousland; penguins diving © Aimee McLachlan; pig © panbazil; pigeon © shuai jie guo; pink dragon millipede © Chatchai Somwat; piranha © Santi Rodriguez; polar bear © Incredible Arctic; polar bear and cubs © Sergey Uryadnikov; praying mantis © Acambium64, Coprid; puffer fish © Kevin H Knuth; puffin © Nicram Sabod; purple sea urchin © NatalieJean; quail © ADA_photo; rabbits © Evgeny Karandaev, Oligo, JIANG HONGYAN; rabbit hopping © Linas T; rainbow lorikeet © jurra8; rat © Pakhnyushcha; red ear turtle © African studio; red Fox © Jeannette Katzir Photog; red panda © feathercollector; red salamander © Cynthia Kidwell; red squirrels © Menno Schaefer; seawhisper © Leon Marais; rhinoceros beetle © PHOTO 999; ring-tailed lemur © Roberto Caucino; roadrunner © Sekar B; robin © Sebastian Knight; salamander © Arun Roisri; scarlet lily beetle © HHelene; sea turtle © Rich Carey; seagulls © Mrs_ya, Yentafern; seahorse © CHEN WS; shark © prochasson frederic; sheep © Vasilyev Alexandr; sheep and lambs © Eric Gevaert; siamese fighting fish © wimammoth; sika deer © Cologne82; slug, woodlouse © schankz; snail © ahnhuynh; snake slithering © bogdan ionescu; snapping turtle © Carol Heesen; snowy owls © O Driscoll Imaging, WayneDuguay; spider © Kondor83; spider in web © papkin; spotted hyena © Aaron Amat; springbok © J Reineke; squirrel © Shane Wilson Link; squirrel monkey © sohadiszno; starfish © Matthew Gough; stick Insect, earwigs © Melinda Fawver; sturgeons © Maxim Petrichuk; swan and babies © Karel Gallas; swan, mouse © Erni; tabby cat © Tompet; tadpoles © Ronald Wilfred Jansen; tarantula © Aleksey Stemmer; tawny owl © Sue Robinson; tiger drinking © Bill Kennedy; tiger salamander © Gerald A. DeBoer; tiger, puma © Dennis Donohue; toucan, squirrel monkey © Eduardo Rivero; vulture © Sue Green; whale shark © Krzysztof Odziomek; white dove © Tischenko Irina; wolf © Kjetil Kolbjornsrud; woodpecker © schaef71; yak © Im Perfect Lazybones; yellow anacondas © cellistka; yellow crab spider © Henrik Larsson; yellow tangs © Chubykin Arkady, Volodymyr Burdiak; zebras © francesco de marco.

All rights reserved. No part of this publication may be reproduced, stored in a retrieval system, or transmitted in any form or by any means, electronic, mechanical, photocopying, recording or otherwise without the prior written permission of the publisher.

Please note that every effort has been made to check the accuracy of the information contained in this book, and to credit the copyright holders correctly. Green Android Ltd apologize for any unintentional errors or omissions, and would be happy to include revisions to content and/or acknowledgements in subsequent editions of this book.

Printed and bound in China, October 2013

Note to parents and carers

Start to Learn Animals is an exciting way to introduce your child to the animal kingdom. Over 500 colourful photographs will encourage your child to browse through the book, recognising familiar animals and discovering new ones.

Help your child learn the names and groups of many kinds of animals by pointing to the clear labels as you name each animal.

Designed as a fun learning experience, Start to Learn Animals will entertain, as well as educate, young children for many hours.

Colourful photography of animals

Challenging interactive questions

Clear labels

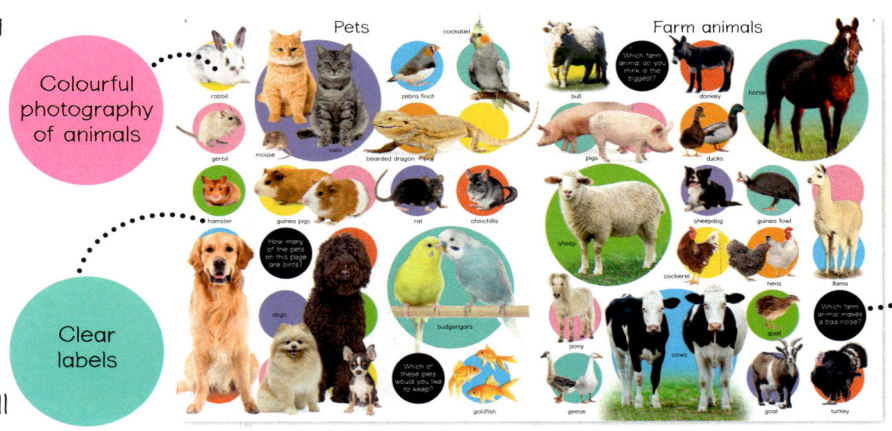

Contents

4 Animal groups

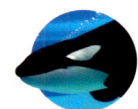

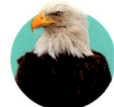

6 Pets

7 Farm animals

8 Minibeasts

10 Giant animals

12 Superb swimmers

14 Birds

16 Scaly animals

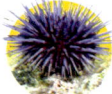

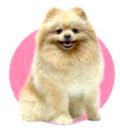

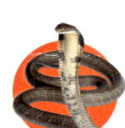

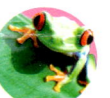

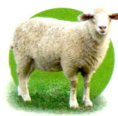

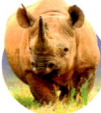

17 Horns, spines and shells

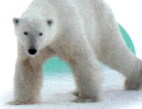

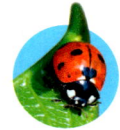

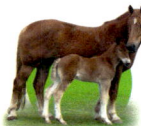

18 Animals and their babies

20 Furry coats

22 Camouflage

24 Colourful animals

26 Frogs and their family

27 Animal homes

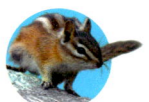

28 Spots and stripes

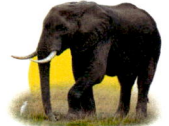

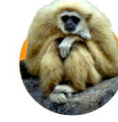

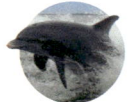

30 Animals in action

32 Index

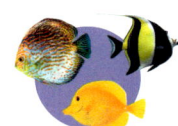

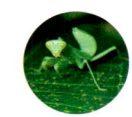

Which is the smallest animal on this page?

Mammals
These warm-blooded animals have lungs to breathe air. They have hair or fur and feed their young with milk.

anteater, elephant, mouse, puma, monkey, oryx, squirrel, orca

Which groups of animals have scales?

Pets

rabbit
gerbil
hamster
mouse
cats
guinea pigs
cockatiel
zebra finch
bearded dragon
rat
chinchilla
dogs
budgerigars
goldfish

How many of the pets on this page are birds?

Which of these pets would you like to keep?

Minibeasts

snail

pond skater

Which minibeast looks most like a leaf?

moth

wasp

leaf insect

Can you find a minibeast that has no legs?

mosquito

spider

fly

stick insect

stag beetle

ladybird

earthworm

lanternfly

ant

Giant animals

hippopotamus

blue whale

Which of these giant animals is a bird?

ostrich

bison

gaur

elephant

brown bear

Which giant animal do you think is the biggest?

Which giant animal has the longest neck?

Which giant animal has two humps on its back?

white rhinoceros

polar bear

moose

crocodile

How many of these giant animals have horns?

walrus

giraffe

camel

Which fish has white and yellow stripes?

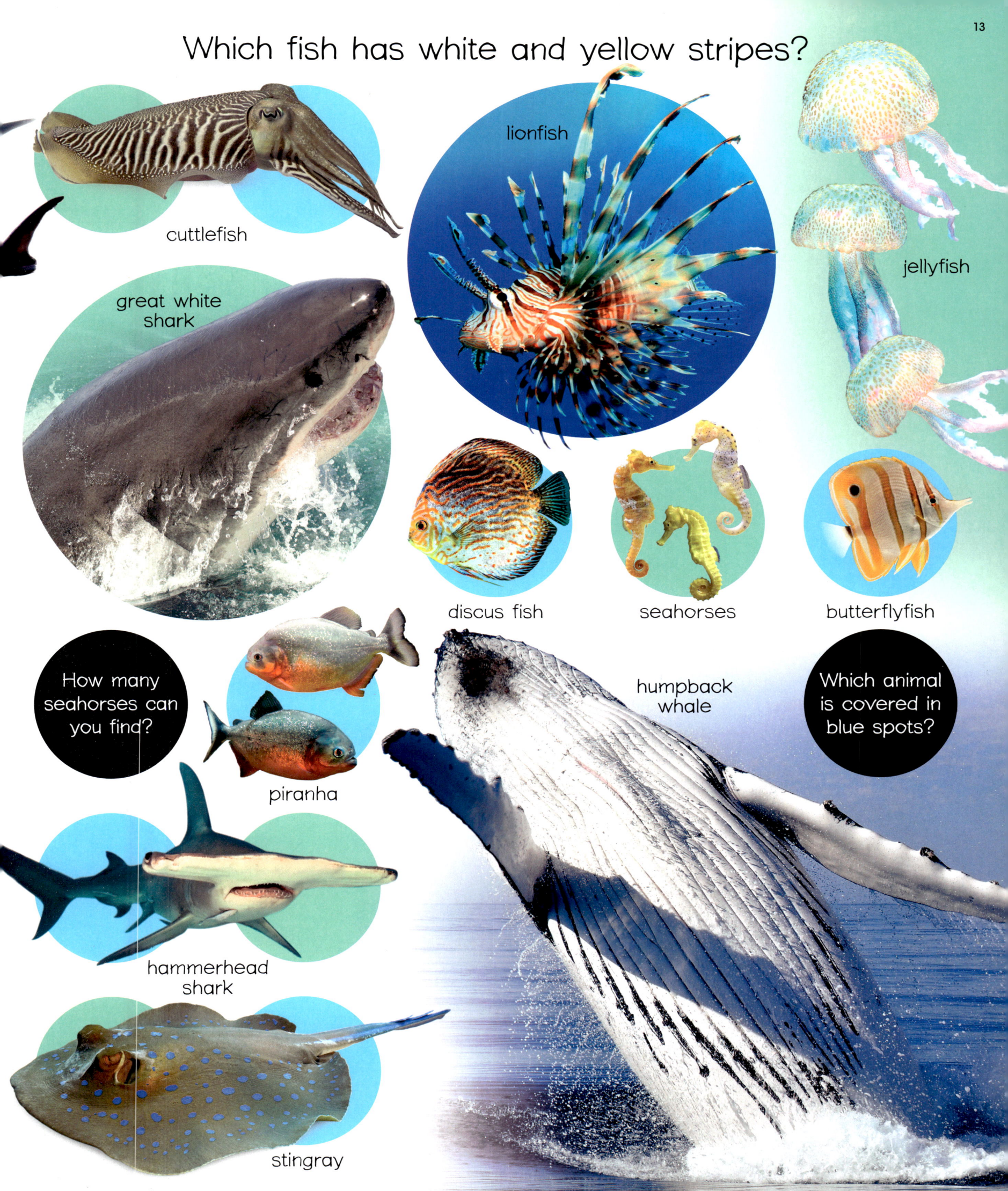

cuttlefish

lionfish

jellyfish

great white shark

discus fish

seahorses

butterflyfish

How many seahorses can you find?

piranha

humpback whale

Which animal is covered in blue spots?

hammerhead shark

stingray

Birds

bald eagle

pelican

blue jay

woodpecker

grey parrot

Which bird has a huge tail of colourful feathers?

seagull

buzzard

toucan

emperor penguin

roadrunner

great horned owl

blue tit

hummingbird

What are the colours on the toucan's beak?

swan

Camouflage

great grey owl on a branch

devil scorpionfish on a reef

gecko in a desert

Which of these animals is hiding in a pond?

eyelash pit viper on a flower

butterfly on the bark of a tree

korhaan walking in grass

Which animal is camouflaged against the sand?

praying mantis on a leaf

leaf mimic katydid among leaves

frog in a pond

Which animal is the hardest to spot?

mossy frog on a tree

partridge in a field

copperhead snake on the forest floor

crab on the seashore

green chameleon in a forest

mountain hare in the snow

arctic fox in the snow

lion in the grassland

Point to the animal hiding on a green leaf.

How many of these animals are birds?

Colourful animals

yellow crab spider

goldfish

Name the colours of all the birds' feathers.

Siamese fighting fish

violet-backed starling

clouded sulphur butterfly

scarlet ibis

blue starfish

pig

caterpillar

Victoria crowned pigeon

Amazon parrot

sea urchin

Which orange fish is often kept as a pet?

red palm weevil

What colour is the spider on this page?

Can you count seven yellow animals on this page?

canaries

sea slug

red squirrel

Where are the two orange orang-utans?

green anole lizard

flamingo

green python

scarlet lily beetle

What two colours appear on the frog's body?

northern cardinal

blue mountain butterfly

yellow tangs

poison dart frog

orang-utan

dragon millipede

How many pink animals can you find?

Frogs and their family

tomato frog

common toad

axolotl

tadpoles

How many toads can you count on this page?

golden poison frog

great crested newt

cane toad

tree frog

harlequin poison frog

crocodile salamander

strawberry poison-arrow frog

Surinam toad

Can you find a frog with two red eyes?

tiger salamander

Amazon milk frog

Spots and stripes

spotted hyena

butterflies

gecko

Where is the butterfly with blue spots?

leopard

bongo

Colorado beetle

ring-tailed lemur

sika deer

leopard frog

Which is the stripy insect on this page?

ladybird

zebra

Animals in action

Index

A
African buffalo 17
Alligator 4, 16
Amazon milk frog 26
Amazon parrot 24
Anaconda 16
Angelfish 29
Ant 4, 8
Anteater 5, 21
Appaloosa horse 29
Arctic fox 22
Armadillo 17
Axolotl 26

B
Badger 29
Bald eagle 14
Bat 27
Bear 10, 11, 20, 27, 30
Bearded dragon 6
Bee 9
Beetle 8, 9, 25, 28, 29, 28
Bison 10
Black rhinoceros 17
Blue jay 14
Blue mountain butterfly 25
Blue tit 14
Blue whale 10
Blue-tongued skink 16
Bobcat 21
Bongo 28
Brown bear 10, 20, 30
Budgerigar 6
Bull 7
Butterfly 9, 22, 24, 25, 28
Butterflyfish 13
Buzzard 14

C
Calf (elephant) 19
Caiman 16
Camel 11
Canary 25
Cane toad 26
Cardinal fish 4
Cat 6, 19
Caterpillar 9, 24, 29
Catfish 4
Centipede 9
Chameleon 16, 17, 23
Cheetah 29, 31
Chick 19
Chimpanzee 20
Chinchilla 6
Chipmunk 29
Clouded sulphur butterfly 24
Clown fish 12
Cockatiel 6
Cockatoo 15
Cockerel 7
Cockroach 9
Collared anteater 21
Collared lizard 16
Colorado beetle 28
Common toad 26
Copperhead snake 23
Corn snake 16
Cow 7
Coyote 21
Crab 17, 23, 24
Crocodile 4, 11
Crocodile salamander 26
Cubs (polar bear) 19
Cuttlefish 13
Cygnets 19

D
Dalmation dog 29
Damselfish 12
Deer 18, 28
Devil scorpionfish 22
Discus fish 13
Dog 6, 18
Dolphin 12, 27, 31
Donkey 7
Dove 4
Dragon millipede 25
Dragonfly 9
Duck 7, 18
Duckling 18
Dung beetle 9

E
Eagle 30
Earthworm 8
Earwig 9
Echidna 17
Eel 12
Elephant 5, 10, 19, 30
Emerald tree boa 16
Emperor penguin 14
Emu 4, 15
Eyelash pit viper 22

F
Fawn 18
Fennec fox 20
Ferret 21
Flamingo 25
Fly 8
Foal 18
Fox 20, 22
Frilled lizard 16
Frog 4, 22, 23, 25, 26, 28, 31

G
Gaur 10
Gecko 22, 28
Geese 7
Gerbil 6
Gibbon 21
Gila monster 16
Giraffe 11, 31
Goat 7, 18
Golden poison frog 26
Goldfish 6, 24
Goose 19
Gorilla 20
Gosling 19
Grasshopper 9
Great crested newt 26
Great grey owl 22
Great horned owl 14
Great white shark 13
Green anole lizard 25
Green chameleon 23
Green python 25
Grey parrot 14
Grey squirrel 21
Grey wolf 21
Guinea fowl 7
Guinea pigs 6

H
Hammerhead shark 13
Hamster 6, 31
Hare 20, 23
Harlequin poison frog 26
Hedgehog 17, 18
Hen 7, 19
Heron 15
Hippopotamus 10
Horse 7, 18, 31
Hummingbird 14
Humpback whale 13

I
Ibex 17
Iguana 16
Impala 20
Indian cobra 16

J
Jackson's chameleon 17
Jaguar 20
Jellyfish 13
Joey 19

K
Kangaroo 19, 30
Kids (goat) 18
Kingfisher 15
Kitten 19
Koala 21
Komodo dragon 16
Kookaburra 15
Korhaan 22

L
Ladybird 8, 28
Lambs 18
Laternfly 8
Leaf insect 8
Leaf mimic katydid 22
Leaf-cutter ant 4
Leafy seadragon 4
Leopard 28
Leopard frog 28
Leopard shark 29
Lion 21, 23, 31
Lionfish 13
Lizard 4, 16, 25
Llama 7
Lobster 17
Lorikeet 15

M
Meerkat 20
Milk snake 29
Millipede 9, 24
Monkey 5
Moorish idol 12
Moose 11
Mosquito 8
Mossy frog 23
Moth 4, 8
Mountain hare 23
Mouse 5, 6, 27
Muskox 20

N
Newt 4, 26
Northern cardinal 25

O
Octopus 12
Okapi 29
Orang-utan 25, 30
Orca 5
Oryx 5
Ostrich 10
Otter 20
Owl 4, 14, 15, 22
Owlet 18

P
Panda 21, 31
Pangolin 16
Partridge 23
Peacock 16
Pelican 14
Penguin 14, 30
Peregrine falcon 15
Pig 7, 24
Pigeon 15, 24
Piglet (hedgehog) 18
Piranha 13
Poision dart frog 25
Polar bear 11, 19, 27
Pond skater 8
Pony 7
Porcupine 17
Praying mantis 9, 23
Puffer fish 12
Puffins 15
Puma 5
Puppies 18

Q
Quail 7

R
Rabbit 6, 19, 27, 30
Rabbit kits 19
Raccoon 21
Rainbow trout 12
Rat 6
Red fox 20
Red palm weevil 24
Red panda 21
Red salamander 29
Red squirrel 25
Rhinoceros 11, 17
Rhinoceros beetle 9
Ring-tailed lemur 28
Roadrunner 14
Robin 15
Royal gramma 4

S
Sailfish 12
Salamander 4, 26, 29
Scarlet ibis 24
Scarlet lily beetle 25
Scorpion 4, 9
Sea lion 12
Sea slug 25
Sea star 24
Sea turtle 12
Sea urchin 24
Seagull 4, 14
Seahorses 13
Shark 4, 12, 13, 29
Sheep 7, 18
Sheepdog 7
Siamese fighting fish 24
Silka deer 28
Skunk 29
Slug 4
Snail 8
Snake 4, 16, 22, 23, 29, 30
Snapping turtle 17
Snowy owl 15
Sparrows 15
Spider 4, 8, 27, 31
Spotted hyena 28
Springbok 31
Squirrel 5, 21, 25, 27
Squirrel monkey 21
Stag beetle 8
Starfish 27
Stick insect 8
Stingray 13
Stork 27
Strawberry poison-arrow frog 26
Sturgeon 12
Surinam toad 26
Swan 14, 19

T
Tadpoles 26
Tangs 12, 25
Tiger 29, 30
Tiger salamander 26
Tigerfish 12
Toad 4, 26
Tomato frog 26
Tortoise 17
Toucan 14
Tree frog 26
Trigger fish 29
Turkey 7
Turtle 4, 12, 17

V
Victoria crowned pigeon 24
Vulture 15

W
Walrus 11
Wasp 8
Whale 10, 13
Whale shark 12
White rhinoceros 11
Wood borer beetle 29
Wood turtle 17
Woodlouse 9
Woodpecker 4, 14

Y
Yak 20
Yellow crab spider 24
Yellow tang 25

Z
Zebra 28
Zebra finch 6